Little Bible Heroes™
Deborah

Written by Victoria Kovacs
Illustrated by David Ryley

B&H KIDS
NASHVILLE, TENNESSEE

GOLDQUILL
WWW.GOLDQUILL.CO.UK

fb.com/littlebibleheroes

Published 2017 by B&H Kids, a division of LifeWay Christian Resources, Nashville, Tennessee.
Text and illustrations copyright © 2017, GoldQuill, United Kingdom.
All rights reserved. Scripture quotations are taken from the Christian Standard Bible ®
Copyright © 2017 by Holman Bible Publishers. Used by permission.
ISBN: 978-1-4627-4336-0   Dewey Decimal Classification: CE
Subject Heading: DEBORAH \ ABIGAIL \ BIBLE STORIES
Printed June 2018 in Shenzhen, Guangdong, China
2 3 4 5 6 7 8 • 22 21 20 19 18

Deborah is a wise judge of Israel. She sits under the Palm Tree of Deborah in the hills. People go to her when they are arguing, and she helps them.

One day, Deborah talks to Barak, an army commander. She tells him, "God wants you to lead His people into battle. Take ten thousand soldiers with you. He will bring you victory over the evil commander Sisera."

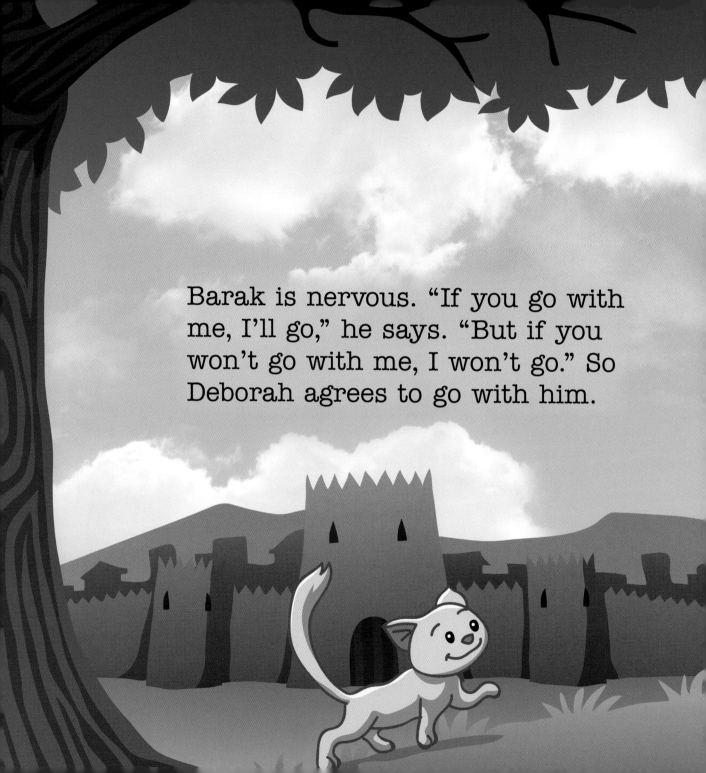

Barak is nervous. "If you go with me, I'll go," he says. "But if you won't go with me, I won't go." So Deborah agrees to go with him.

Sisera is a strong enemy. His army has nine hundred iron chariots. But Deborah knows that God is on her side!

Barak gathers his soldiers.
He and Deborah are ready
for battle.

Deborah tells Barak, "This is the day when God will help you defeat Sisera!"

God causes Sisera and his army to be confused. Deborah and Barak win the battle!

They sing a song of praise to thank God.

Read:

I will sing to the Lord; I will sing praise to the Lord God of Israel.—Judges 5:3

Think:

1. How did God help Deborah and Barak?
2. Deborah sang a song to thank God. What are some ways you thank God when He helps you?

Remember:

God loves to help you!

Read:

Then David said to Abigail, "Blessed be the LORD God of Israel, who sent you to meet me today!"—1 Samuel 25:32

Think:

1. Do you like to share? When is it hard?
2. Why does God want us to be kind to others?

Remember:

God is kind, and He wants us to be kind too.

Abigail says yes and
becomes David's bride.

Later, David hears that Nabal has died. He remembers wise Abigail and asks her to marry him.

David is not mad anymore.

Abigail bows to David and gives him all the food. She asks for his forgiveness and says, "Remember me."

Abigail is smart. She loads lots of food and drink on donkeys and hurries to find David.

David is very mad. He wants to kill Nabal. A servant tells Abigail what happened.

One day, David sends messengers to ask Nabal for food and drink. But Nabal is too mean. He won't share with David.

Abigail is a smart, beautiful woman. She is married to Nabal. He owns three thousand sheep and a thousand goats. He is very rich but very rude.

Little Bible Heroes™
Abigail

Written by Victoria Kovacs
Illustrated by David Ryley

BYH KIDS
NASHVILLE, TENNESSEE

GOLDQUILL
WWW.GOLDQUILL.CO.UK

fb.com/littlebibleheroes

Published 2017 by B&H Kids, a division of LifeWay Christian Resources, Nashville, Tennessee.
Text and illustrations copyright © 2017, GoldQuill, United Kingdom.
All rights reserved. Scripture quotations are taken from the Christian Standard Bible ®
Copyright © 2017 by Holman Bible Publishers. Used by permission.
ISBN: 978-1-4627-4336-0   Dewey Decimal Classification: CE
Subject Heading: DEBORAH \ ABIGAIL \ BIBLE STORIES
Printed June 2018 in Shenzhen, Guangdong, China
2 3 4 5 6 7 8 • 22 21 20 19 18